Orsamus Charles Dake

Nebraska Legends and Poems

Orsamus Charles Dake

Nebraska Legends and Poems

ISBN/EAN: 9783337155650

Printed in Europe, USA, Canada, Australia, Japan

Cover: Foto ©Thomas Meinert / pixelio.de

More available books at **www.hansebooks.com**

NEBRASKA LEGENDS.

1

NEBRASKA LEGENDS

AND

POEMS

BY

ORSAMUS CHARLES DAKE

POTT & AMERY,
COOPER UNION, NEW YORK.
1871.

THE NEW YORK PRINTING COMPANY,
205, 207, 209, 211, 213 EAST 12TH STREET

TO MY EVER CLOSE COMPANION
AND THE BLESSING OF MY LIFE,
TO THE MOTHER OF MY CHILDREN,
TO MY WIFE,
BE INSCRIBED THIS LITTLE VOLUME ;
AH, MIGHT IT BECOME A COLUMN
SURE AS BRONZE OR FLINTY MARBLE,
TO OUTLAST THE AGES SOLEMN,
IT SHOULD PROVE HOW MUCH I OWE HER
AND A NAME DESERVED BESTOW HER.

1*

PREFACE.

THESE poems are tentative, both of my own strength and of the public taste. They have been produced at a point remote from literary fellowship, where I have been thrown solely on my own judgment. My surroundings and the incidents of life have suggested them all. Possibly I may hereafter touch them into fairer proportion after hearing the views of competent critics.

In the development of the two Nebraska legends I have treated my Indian characters as noble, and possessed of a true sentiment. A brutal savage is not a poetical object, and, except under rare conditions, has no business in poetry. If the Indian, like his human brethren of more favorable opportunities, has his worse side, he also has his better. Until corrupted by intercourse with the whites, his nature was simple, affectionate, childlike. Certainly he is no worse than the old pagan Greeks of Homer and the Dramatists, who were separated into little tribes, forever at war, and whose common occupation was the sacking of towns and the carrying off of defenceless women for concubines. Every inducement, therefore, that could urge an ancient poet to portray prehistoric peoples as chivalrous and of a sustained dignity, should impel the writer of to-day to do likewise. Elemental poetic conditions do not change.

Should time and space be granted me, I hope, at no distant day, to again make trial of the public favor. Certain ideas, originated by social aspects, have long lain in my mind, and I should be glad to work them into a poem. This, however, must depend upon the time and strength snatched from duties of a more practical kind.

FREMONT, NEBRASKA, *September* 20, 1870.

CONTENTS.

PAGE

PREFACE 7

THE WEEPING WATER 11

THE RAW HIDE 53

THE PRAISE OF NEW LANDS 75

NEBRASKA IN 1866 89

THE MISSOURI 93

GRAPING 97

THE DEATH OF THE STAG 103

TO THE SOUTH WIND 105

RALLYING SONG—1864 111

THE UNKNOWN SAIL AT NANTUCKET 113

FAIR AND FRAIL 117

THE FORGOTTEN POET 121

                                                    PAGE
To Zephyr 123

Misther O'Flanagan's Advoise til a Cunthryman . 125

Longing   129

Nebraska, Dear Nebraska   131

Lothair   135

Magdalen   137

RELIGIOUS POEMS.

Aspiration   149

Sad Heart, Sow in Tears 151

It Matters Not   153

Christmas Eve—1869 157

Religious Divisions   159

THE WEEPING WATER.

THE Omaha and Otoe Indians, being at war, chanced to meet on their common hunting-ground south of the Platte River, in Nebraska. A fierce battle ensued, in which all the male warriors of both tribes being slain, the women and children came upon the battle-field and sat down and wept. From the fountain of their tears arose and ever flows the little stream known as Ne-hawka, or the Weeping Water.

I.

The lingering suns crept round a land at peace,
While June, warm-eyed, was loitering in the vales.
Long-gone was seed-time ; and the sportive birds
Flew through broad-bladed corn, or 'mid the bloom
Of yellow melon-flowers, where slope the fields
Down to the Elkhorn stream.

                  But there was one
Among the Otoe lodges on the bluffs
Full envious of the mated cheerful birds—
He, Sananona named, o' the Iron Eyes.
Who, dreaming long in virtuous discontent
For that the summer kindled in his blood
And all his life grew languorous for his love,
Came with the sunrise to the wealthy lodge
Of his sole chief, Shosguscan. Him he found
Sitting without, on soft Cayoté robes—

     1

One idle hand with a pet dog a-toy,

And in his mouth his pipe of blood-red stone.

Mutely expectant, then, the young man stood,

While grim Shosguscan, with half-opened eyes,

Looked subtly in the tell-tale, wishful face,

'Gainst which the level sunbeams pushed their spears ;

But all was silent save the sighing wind.

At length the sage chief spoke : " It is no foe

Lurking amidst our corn-fields, nor wise thought

Of public welfare brings thee here, I see.

What wouldst thou, Sananona ? "

                          As when first

A school-boy, trapped in frivolous mischief, writhes

Like a hurt worm beneath the master's eye,

But, finding no excuse, confesses all,

Young Sananona, glancing right and left,

Abashed and humbled thus to tell his love,

Unveiled his heart.

                " Mine are the wants of youth,

Oh, great Shosguscan—youth, thou knowest, has wants.

To be the victor in all manly sports,

To tireless chase the flying antelope,

To battle all day long with worthy foes—

These are youth's wants : but youth has wants besides.

On windy nights I sit within my door

Voiceless and lonely, for I lack a mate.

Small need is mine to hunt the shaggy bull,

Or lure the wary pickerel from the lake—

Success is bootless where it is unshared."

Here grim Shosguscan, with impatient yawn—

" Oh ! Ah ! Well, take a wife ! "

               " That would I do,"

Quoth Sananona.

             " And what hinders then ? "

Shosguscan cried. " Go, make deliberate choice

Among our dark-eyed girls, and her lead home

That best befits your mind ! And wherefore here ?

Why speak to me of maids, and windy nights,

And sentimental loneliness ? Not I—

I am no tier of true-lovers' knots,

No go-between for billing boys and girls,

No dealer in love-simples for sore hearts.

I hold myself for something different.

I am a warrior, Sananona, I—

A man of mighty battles and of blood.

Mine is the voice of wisdom in our tribe—

The hand that guides and rules.   Not me for love,

Not me for maidens seek ; but find some crone

That, as a quacking duck along the streams,

Leads forth her timorous brood ! Go ! Go ! young man,

From women seek your mate ! "

      Against this scorn

Wrathful and black young Sananona stood.

But as before his nation's chief befits

A youth to stand with quiet modesty

And humbled self-importance, so he paused

To smother impulse and select his words.

" I am not here to seek your offices,

Oh, brave Shosguscan, as a go-between.

I ask no man to win a maid for me.

I best can tell the secret I best know.

But this my errand : she who has my heart,

And whom with pure and honorable rites
I would install as mistress of my lodge,
Is not an Otoe ; dwells not by the stream
Of the swift Elkhorn ; but among the tents
Of warlike Omahas—a handsome race—
She honors womanhood and waits for me.
Her tribesmen know our troth, and are content."

"So you would bring a foreign woman here ! "
Cried harsh Shosguscan. " One who, in the days
Of vigilant warfare, shall forewarn her friends,
Bringing defeat to counsel :—one whose heart
Shall evermore be flying to the fields
Wherein her childhood played, and to the light
Of kindly faces she may see no more.
Have Otoe maidens, then, no amorous grace ?
The daughters of your fathers,—are they worse
Or less attractive than this alien girl ?
Why shame your people thus ? "

                Then gravely spoke
The Iron-Eyed : " I cannot read my heart

To say why this I choose, why that reject.

I follow love's blind instinct.   If I err,

Mine is the error common to our race.

But love that blindly leads is seldom wrong,

For most are happy in their wedded loves.

Indifferent I see our Otoe girls ;

But when Nacoumah, in the April days,

I met among her people, then my heart

Rose up and followed after.   Oh, my chief,

Respect my hopes, I pray, and bid me go

To hither bring the maiden of the North,

And I, in times of danger, with my life

Will answer for her loyalty ! "

                                               Then stood

The youth expectant, pleading with his face

That mirrored forth the hopes and fears within,

As the great Platte, when low in autumn days

Near to its islands on its glassy wave

Reveals the woodlands and the forest-life.

And stern Shosguscan, musing on his face

And running over all the honored past,

When Sananona, in the thickest fight,

Had borne the brunt of battle with the best,

And wrought great deeds, and won the hearts of all,

Wavered, inclined to grant his moving suit,

And bid him seek his maid and bring her home.

But swift succeeded thoughts of what was best

For general welfare, and the answer he

Not for himself, led by a yielding heart,

But for his tribe should make.   Then thus he said :

" Oh, Sananona, much I long to yield

This boyish quest, for I, too, have been young.

I know how whimsical this youthful love—

With what caprices unaccountable

The youth selects his maid, the maid her man.

I know how disappointment pricks, and how

The heart, defeated of its cherished aim,

Knots its great arteries and swells with sighs

And strives to burst.   And I would spare all pain :

But this I know—for I, too, have been young—

That love has lives as many as the bear,

That, being filled with arrows and with spears,

'Scapes to the hills, plucks forth the barbs, and grows,

Erelong, as vigorous as before.   To-day,

None like Nacoumah : but ere wintry suns

Waste nebulous glances in the frozen gales,

Some other maiden will inspire your sighs ;

For youth runs lightly into any love.

Oh, be advised !   Go seek an Otoe bride.

Dismiss this passion ; it will work your bale—

Nor you alone, but all.   Go ! ”

                    And he went.

Straight to his lodge the young brave went, and closed

His door, and with himself communed.   As one

Who, whirling through the country by a train

That flies the track and plunges down a steep,

Picks himself out from shattered heaps of cars

And smutched and mangled bodies of the dead ;

Then feels along each bruised limb with care,

And slowly breathes to test if hurts within

Threaten life's citadel ; so all his heart

Sad Sananona to himself exposed,

And weighed Nacoumah 'gainst the Otoe girls,

And said, at length, " No other wife for me

But she who has my heart! This argument

Shosguscan holds about a light-heeled love

That dances like a reed-blade in the wind

Hither and thither, without settled bound,

Suits him, perhaps—not me. Come then what may :

If brief my life, it now is summer-time,

And a few sun-bright days of well-placed love

I stake against the wrath of all my tribe.".

So, sauntering to the valley with a line

As one on pensive piscatory bent,

Soon as the woodlands hid his stealthy course

He northward turned, and sought and found his bride.

II.

And days went by—the laughing days of June :

But yet the Otoe was supplied with meat

And wrought no havoc with the flocks of God,

But let the days in aimless waste go by

Amid his wives in the well-furnished lodge,

Content with peace,—with idleness and peace.

1*

But when, at length, the women raised a wail

Of shortening substance and the grim-eyed wolf,

He rose, as one from sleep, and felt his strength—

Stretching his sinews in the pleasant sun.

And as an eagle whets his murderous beak

Upon the tree-top and the granite-ledge,

Or practises in cloud-land his fell swoop,

When, dropping from immeasurable heights

A thousand fathoms down, we see him first

A speck in the abyss, then soars and falls,

Rises and sinks again and yet again,

Each time descending lower, until, at last,

He hovers o'er his nest and settles there,

The hunter filed his flinty arrow-heads,

Sharpened the hatchet and the dreadful knife,

And day by day bent to athletic games—

To run long miles, to leap a miry brook,

To shoot a reed-mark, and to overthrow

His mighty tribesmen in the wrestler's toils,

Winning great fame, and mastering his powers,

Until, fatigued, at evening home was sweet.

But when the moon was rounding night by night,

And the green hills were flooded with its bath

Of silver-streaming light, through which far swam

The sentinel eye—distrustful of surprise—

The Otoe passed the threshold of his lodge

In the great village on the Elkhorn bluffs,

Called forth his thronging progeny and wives,

And wended to the south.

          So fared they forth—

The inspiration of necessity

Their constant guide—as through long ages, back

To the abnormal hour that bore to time

Their changeless race.   But aptly framed their rules

For a rude justice, and the lack of law

Custom, the precedent of use, supplied.

Among their bands no daft reformer rose

To paint the visions of his flighty soul,

And lead to lands hung toppling in the air,

But childlike and content they held and taught,

Without abridgment or an added grain,

The simple faith their fathers left to them—

Growing a rock-firm habit in their race.

So went they forth, as went in all past years,

And as still go in the deep spirit-world,

Their awful fathers and their lovely wives,

When on their annual hunts.   The van was led

By a well-chosen band of warriors, proved

On many a nameless but death-smitten field.

These, mounted on swift steeds—swift as the clouds,

Low-hung outriders of a coming storm—

Armed at all points with bow and lofty lance,

And murderous hatchet and the gleaming knife,

Rode dreadful on the hills or through the vales,

Scanning each shadow for a foe.   Much need

For caution was there.   On these hunting-grounds

The fearful Sioux were oft in battle met.

As when along some blown Alaskan vale

A herd of Caribou drags forth its length,

Seeking for mosses underneath the snow,

And at the front its antlered patriarchs

Explore the route and lead the hinds and young,

That, feeding, follow happy and secure.

Behind them streamed the families with their goods,

Women and children loitering by the way,

Ponies with tent-poles dragging at their sides,

And the gaunt pack that bays the midnight moon.

And all day long before them fled the game

Across the pleasant plains, or stood and eyed

From some low eminence of rounded hill

With timid curiosity.

And thus

Two days they journeyed to the south and west,

A June-time journey in a June-time mood,

And sport and love and laughter ruled the time.

But now was reached a fair idyllic land—

A land of rolling meadow, and of rills

That rippled through the morning like a voice,

Or filled the darkness with mysterious sighs.

Then, as ere eve the chief decreed to camp,

With noisy clamor, as a flock of crows,

That, lighting, huddle round a lonely marsh,

Some kindle fires and cook the generous meal

Of savory antelope, or prairie-hen,

Or rabbit, freshly caught; and some brace fast

The lofty lodge-poles o'er an ample space,

And fold them deep in warmth-compelling skins.

The women, as befits domestic ways,

Spread the wide couch of soft and well-tanned robes—

Beaver, or otter, or the delicate fawn ;

And children stand beside the glowing fires,

Babbling between their mouthfuls with full hands.

But ere the tasks were ended, or the feast

Palled on a dulled and sated appetite,

From out the hollow valleys of the south

Rose tawny mists of smoke, and clomb to heaven,

And caught the sunset in wan flowing horns.

Then all the women were aware of fear,

But every man felt at his mighty heart

A sterner pulsing, for his will was firm.

And, as an oak that bears the rushing storm,

And quakes not at the thunder in its strength,

But gnarls and knots in stubborn pride of power,

So grew his muscles tense and hard as twist—

Conditioned for a conflict, must it come.

But, as a brood of wild-cats, when a dog,

Snuffing along the woodlands, nears their nest,

Gather at once around the faithful dam,

The Otoe tribesmen hasten to the lodge

Of brave Shosguscan. Him alone they found

Sitting before his tent; a massive soul,

And clear of vision as the morning star.

Wisdom and will spoke from his lordly face—

A presence that bends others without words—

Incarnate manhood's just authority.

Thus as he sat, his blinkless eye full-fixed

Upon the smoke-wreaths whirling o'er the hills,

Around him came in silence and sat down

His warlike tribesmen : but no word they spoke.

Long-time he mused. At length the deep-toned voice

Rose as a full-brimmed bucket from a well,

Lifting its treasure for men's needs.

                    " Ye men

Of Otoe, conscious in our strength to stand

Unflinching in the face of every foe,

And in the fiercest battle to maintain
Our right, we wander through these hunting-grounds
As inclination leads.   If any doubt
Our purpose of free action, or our power
To hold a ground once taken, let them come
And put constraint upon us, bit our mouths,
And tame us, as a horse, to know the rein,
Or drive us homewards, as a fox is sped
Back to its cover.   In the face of all
We sit down here.   We seek no fight, indeed,
Nor do we seek to shun one.   For this night
Put forth a double line of sentinels,
And let the Otoes sleep upon their arms."

But, as the brave Shosguscan finished thus,
An Omaha, that, hunting through the hills,
Had from afar surveyed the Otoe camp
And recognized the tribe by many signs,
Came in with friendly words, and straightway told
How his own tribe were also on the hunt,
And two days earlier wandered to the south,

And had success with buffalo and deer :

That theirs the camps deep in the hollow vales,

Whose fires had wreathed the sunset in a robe

Of tinted mist. So, then, no thought remained

Of foes and war ; but, as a man derives

In difficult places from a true friend's face

Support and confidence and heedless ease,

These neighbor-tribes, now for a time at peace—

Equal in numbers and resource of war—

Felt each securer in the other's might.

But on the morrow Sananona, who

A fortnight had been strayed, was hailed by friends

And Otoe comrades straggled for pastime

Among the Omahas, as he was seen

With sweet Nacoumah, now his wedded wife.

And straightway these, with garrulous speech at home

Discoursing of the pair, their secret soon

Touched at Shosguscan's ear.   And for that he—

Judicial even in his social moods—

Never forgave a personal affront

Or question of opinion, but was stern,

And, as the ice upon a wintry stream,

Cold and inflexible ; forthwith he sent

Two valiant warriors, creatures of his own,

To summon Sananona from his bride,

And bid him haste to his paternal chief,

Who for his absence felt a deep concern.

But Sananona, with shrewd speech, declined.

Too well he guessed the great obnoxious paw

Of the fierce panther, that o'ertakes the herds

Among the mountain valleys by the Platte,

Was lighter than his chief's official hand.

But, as the Otoe heralds homeward turned,

He to his new-made friends and kinsmen ran,

And, gathering them—a listening group—apart,

Thus spoke : " O friends, O brethren, now—for such

To me ye are, since he who weds a wife

Becomes more surely member of her house

Than she of his—I claim your aid to-day.

When first I saw Nacoumah, my cold heart—

That in its chamber dragged a numb, dead life,

As, in some hollow trunk through wintry days

Pent by the frigid darkness, clings the bee—

Flew, like the bee in Spring-time, when the breast

Of the broad prairie sparkles into bloom

With flowers of every hue, and found in her

Its treasure and its rest. With your consent,

Her have I taken in all proper rites

To share my lodge and life. But skies grow foul.

This very hour Shosguscan, my tribe's chief,

By embassy sent secretly to me,

Commands my presence at his lodge, intent

To force me from my bride. Stern, harsh is he—

Inflexible, and lightly holds youth's love.

Now would he widow her whom I have wed,

And punish preference that goes from home.

But you, good friends, I know your generous will,

Your courage, and your might. And more I know;

I know you honor natural love and grief,

And hate oppression that has no excuse.

Be with me, then, I pray, in this dire strait,

Nor let the chief Shosguscan snatch me hence!

Much do I fear, lest coming with a band

Of sturdy warriors trained to work his will,

He seize me suddenly.   That danger past,

We may conclude this matter happily

In council, tribe with tribe."

                Forthwith replied

Nacoumah's uncle, chief Watonashie—

Watonashie, among the Omahas

Highest in rank : " O Sananona, hear !

No harm shall reach you without due offence.

I, these our kinfolk, all our warlike tribe,

Will take due care that bold Shosguscan comes

Not here, nor plays at force near us, unless—

Indeed," and now Watonashie looked grave

As one abstracted in a passing thought,

And fingered with his mighty hand the plumes

Fixed in the tough, smooth handle of his spear—

" Unless, indeed, he try a game of war,

And do his worst, and hazard all."

                Thus, then,

The Omahas, alert to aid the youth

Whose fault seemed but the natural human way,

Stood forth to champion him 'gainst his own tribe,

And kept a wary watch.

Meanwhile the two

Sent by Shosguscan for the Iron-Eyed

Came empty-handed back and told their tale.

Then from his seat wrathful Shosguscan rose—

Zealous for his despised authority—

And, gathering a score of stalwart braves

Strode o'er the hills and neared the wealthy tents

Of the stout-hearted Omahas.   And, when

Not turning right or left, as bent to work

Only his errand and no parley hold,

He pushed direct for Sananona's lodge,

Sudden, across his pathway, shot a bar—

Large-limbed Watonashie and warriors fierce,

A host, who never turned away from war.

So then Watonashie : " Friend, wherefore here ?

What means this show of force ?   This is no place

To venture in rude guise of war."

As when

A gaunt wolf, wandering near the guarded folds,

Falls in a trap of close serrated steel,

And, stung by pain and maddened in his mind

Pulls at the chain and tests the firm trap's strength,

But, mastered, yields at last, the Otoe chief

Paused in the presence of superior force,

His keen eye flashing forth impatient wrath,

And thus replied : " I come to claim my right.

Great chief, you know me well.   Within your tents

There lurks one Sananona, who is mine.

For him alone I come.   No blade of grass

That's yours would we disturb.   We ask our own—

Just that.   Give me the hiding fugitive,

And let our tribes be friends as heretofore."

Then spoke Watonashie, great-hearted chief:

" Young Sananona is, indeed, with us,

And wedded to a maiden of our blood—

Nacoumah, niece of mine.   A nobler pair

Were never matched ;—he, tall and lithe of form

As panther bred 'mid Black Hill spines, and she
Soft as the moonlight of a night in May.
Much do I love them—I who have no sons
Or daughters, childless chief. So I do pray
If Sananona, for some venial fault,
Has merited your wrath, this timely day
You speak his pardon and receive his thanks,
And make him happy in his sweet-faced bride—
For his sake and for mine.ˊ So shall there be
Peace and a happy auspice for both tribes."

But promptly sage Shosguscan answered him :
" This youth, great chief, for whom you plead so well,
With headstrong purpose and for boyish whim
Has broken rule, and furnished precedent
To other youths and maids and sturdy braves
To scorn authority. In every tribe
Order stands only in obedience ;
And he who rules soon loses just respect
If culprits may escape unscathed. So now
I cannot fault like his condone. All men

Have friends to plead in their excuse ; and faults,

Beginning small, pass quickly on to worse.

Confusions come, and anarchy and hate.

A fountain, as it rises, may be choked,

But none can quell a river."

              Slowly, then,

Watonashie, as one half-musing, said :

" How much man prizes selfish sovereignty.

He makes a rule accordant with his thought,

And none shall break it with impunity.

The happiness of units is a toy

Weighed 'gainst a chief's command.   This is not well.

Better relax a rule, than break a heart

Where no crime is."   And then he paused, as one

Who offers opportunity of speech.

But silence reigned ; no word the Otoe chief

Uttered ; but stood defiant in his post,

As one who will not yield.   Then to his height

The mighty-limbed Watonashie drew up

His length enormous, and his fearful hand,

Bony and vast, with threatening gesture raised,

And flashed his furious eyes like shooting-stars,

And in a voice of winter thunder cried,

" He you seek, hard-hearted warrior, sits

At ease within my tent.   Go, take him now :

Go, take him if you can ; but, ere you go,

Weigh well the outcome.   You shall bite the dust

Sooner than he, unless my might prove less

Than yours : of that make trial when you will ! "

To him Shosguscan, with a baleful face,

But calmly, answered : " Do not doubt that I

Will take young Sananona from your tent.

I will not yield the right, except to force

I am unequal to oppose."   So, then,

He turned, and with him went the Otoe braves

Back o'er the hills, and sought the Otoe tents.

Then did Watonashie, restraining those

Who longed to slay Shosguscan where he stood,

Or chase him homeward like a flying stag,

Gather together all the chiefs and braves

2

Among the Omahas, and council hold
And war-like preparation make.

                    So, too,
Shosguscan called his Otoe warriors forth,
And bade them summon up their utmost might,
And fail not to avenge their chief's affront.

But when next morning, timorous and cold,
Flushed o'er the east like one who, half-awake,
Unfolds a drowsy eye, puts forth an arm,
And takes the glimmering prospect of his room,
The Otoe and the Omaha, well-armed,
Banded for fight and swept across the hills—
Seeking, not waiting, for the foe.   And as
Along that green and dewy-gleaming land
The level sunrise streamed an amber flood,
The very prairies seemed to move and slip,
As in an earthquake.   Host drew near to host,
Masses opaque, swart, thundering on fierce steeds,
Or running with fleet foot.   'Gainst the low sun
Their cold spears glittered like a snow-glazed plain,

Brandished with threats and hate.   Then with a crash.
As when in August-storms, among the bluffs
Above the Platte, or on its heated plain,
Reverberating thunders peal and bound,
The fierce tribes met, and each to each with whoop
Answered—whoop dire as shriek of hopeless fiends
Weltering upon the surges of remorse.

Then deeds of daring might were done, and hosts
Battled for sovereign rites, and for the laws
Of hospitality.   The vanquished asked
No quarter; none the victors gave.   The war
Was no pretence, no hollow sham disguised,
To gain a footing for diplomacy;
But every blow meant death, and death rejoiced
And spread his bloody meshes wide for all.
But Sananona, who from far had watched
The progress of the battle, and the death
Of many warriors saw, turned, sick at heart
And moaning in his grief, and sought the tent
That hid his bride, Nacoumah.   Her he found

Engaged in sweet domestic ways, alone

In the wide tent.   Within his arm her waist

He drew, and fondly kissed her beauteous cheek,

And wept, and said, " Farewell, dear bride, farewell.

My time has come ; the tribes too long have fought ;

Too long death ravened on the innocent—

And I sole cause of war.   But if I die

No need of battle or of blood remains.

No other family must forever mourn

For my offence, or all will curse my name,

And in the coming times will haply say,

' He loved himself; he lived and saw the sun,

But had no will to spare the braves who died,

No pity on their children or their wives.' "

And him Nacoumah answered through her tears :

" Dear, noble heart, go, battle with our friends ;

Go do great deeds, and win a name for me.

Why speak of death ?   The grave is dark and foul—

Forgotten soon, and no man loves the grave.

Have I no charms ? and care you not to see

Your prattling children playing at the door

Of the dear lodge ?   O speak no more of death."

But he replied : " I am not left to choose

Or life or death, the arms of wife and babe,

Or the fierce worm.   Fate has made choice for me.

Through all last night, while you slept at my side,

A shadow, with moon-eyes and chilly touch

Stood over me, and breathed, in hollow voice,

' Come, Sananona, come : the grave is made,

The worm awaits ! '   But just at morning light

A sun-bright figure with a happy face

Displaced the bodiless spectre of the night,

And told me that to-day my life shall be

Far, far away, among the prairie-hills

And blooming valleys of the land of souls.

I go to meet my fate ; but I shall look

Athwart the gates of morning year by year,

And peer in every coming woman's face,

Matron or maiden, hoping e'er for you.

Farewell, dear bride, farewell."

                So in the long

And painful rapture of a last embrace,

They clung with tears and bitter, aching hearts,

Till Sananona, summoning his strength,

His sweet Nacoumah's fond arms disengaged,

Put on the stolid look an Indian wears,

And turned away and sought the bloody field.

Where fiercest strained the fight he came, and cried,

"Hold, Otoes, Omahas, ye warriors brave!

No further need is there of blood and hate.

I come to end this cruel war, and save

Your women's eyes from tears, your babes from want.

Live you, but let me die—mine the war's cause,

Mine be its latest wo.   But you henceforth

Be friends!"

      Then from the conflict paused the hosts

At gaze, while Sananona, well-beloved

By either tribe, fixed in the yielding soil

The polished handle of his keen-edged spear,

And pulled aside his robe, and bared his breast,

And fell upon the spear-point.   Straight it drove

To his brave heart, and the hot blood was seen,

And he fell backwards, like a bird that flies

Against the wires suspended in mid-air

On poles of inland telegraphs, and died.

But a wan cloud, that in the midmost heaven

Had gathered unperceived in the sun's path,

Sent forth a frightful wail of frightened winds

And scattered tearful drops, and, from its edge

Sulphureous, whirled a luminous, hissing bolt,

Along whose wake the thunder cracked and roared

Above the hosts.   Great horror fell on all.

But the cloud slipped away into thin air,

The sweet wild winds sang a sweet song of June,

And the sun shone.

          Then to the Omahas

Shosguscan said : " Why do we stand at war ?

The end I sought is reached ; due penalty

Exacted from the insubordinate.

Had I myself for Sananona's fault

Awarded punishment, his life, no doubt,

Would be untouched.   But now I do rejoice

That he, by his own act, before you all

His blame confesses and my sentence spares.

In after years, when these vast hosts are gone,

And other warriors roam these flowery plains,

It shall be told by many an evening fire,

For youth's instruction, how this young man brought

Two peaceful tribes to fearful chance of war,

And compassed his own death by headlong lust

That mocked at duty.   Sananona's name

Shall then be synonym of scorn of law,

Of disobedience.   So others all,

By his sad fate and this brief war forewarned,

Shall settle to their places with content,

And just authority no more be spurned.

Now let the calumet be lit and passed,

And Omaha and Otoe be sure friends,

As heretofore."

    But stout Watonashie,

Turning half-way to his own men, replied :

" 'Twixt me and that fierce wolf can be no peace !

What was this Sananona's fault ?   His fault ?—

He wed a daughter of the Omaha,

Nacoumah, whom I, childless, love as well

As if she were my own.   For this alone—

Because he followed where love's instinct led,

And prized the natural hunger of the heart

As something better than a beast's desire,

As all too sacred for another's will

To guide or thwart, he lies here dead to-day.

But now this crafty chief, Shosguscan, he

Who is at blame for all this bloody work,

Would point a moral with the young man's name—

Victim of pitiless vengeance—and ourselves

Having dishonored by this show of war,

From which he gains his end, would pause and smoke

The Peace-Pipe in a handsome covenant,

And crawl away, himself secure from harm.

This must not be !   Good friends, it shall not be !

My arm aches for reprisal, and my will

Exacts from battle yon disturber's blood.

No talk of peace be here ! "

              Then flew the spears ;

The barbed sharp arrows hissed along the air,

And the hot hosts strained to death's furious work.

As when along the bottoms by the streams

    2*

In Autumn, when the dense tall grass is dry,

Two surging fires, by opposite currents driven,

Eat all before them over untold miles,

And leave behind no thick tall spire of grass,

Or tough brown weed, but charred black clumps of roots,

Unsightly, on the desolated fields,

So all day long, through feverish hours of noon,

Till the great sun lay low above the hills,

The adverse hosts each through the other whirled,

And death made brutal havoc, and the field

Was black and bloody with the fallen dead.

But as the sun, descending, touched the hills,

And the last breath of winds that die away

With sunset sighed across the world, two chiefs—

One Omaha, one Otoe, now the sole

Survivors of that brave, infuriate day—

Bleeding with many wounds, but black with hate,

Drew to each other o'er the slippery field.

Then spoke Watonashie: "Shosguscan, fiend,

I joy to meet thee thus; come, find thy death;

And by the evening fire in after times

It shall be told their children by the old

How Sananona died for hapless love,

Forbidden by his chief; and also how

The fierce Shosguscan, who held hearts as cheap,

And felt no sympathy with others' pain,

Destroyed two tribes entire, and died himself

And left his carcass to the croaking crows."

To him Shosguscan, weary with his wounds,

And sick at heart for all his warriors slain,

Yet full of wrath, " I know that death is near,

Nor would I live, survivor sole and sad

Of all I mourn.   For them alone I lived ;

With them 'tis sweet to die.   I stood to-day

A champion of authority and law,

But thou of wilfulness and anarchy.

And both have lost.   But I would fight again

This dreadful fray, and sacrifice, besides,

The tender mother and her prattling child,

Unconscious of my thought, rather than yield

This cause.   I could not brook that each should be

An individual law, for turbulence

And personal assertion, more than death,

I dread.   But thou, Watonashie, stand forth !

The hour demands far else than braggart words,

For I am proved in battle, and have seen

Thy whole tribe fall.   Thou, too, shalt die ; the sun

Shall never look upon thy face again

Living.   Now share thy tribesmen's fate ! "

                                 As when

Upon the broad, smooth current of a stream,

Two iron rams, with long, steel-pointed beaks,

Lunge at each other's sides, or sterns, or keels

Below the water-line, seeking some place

Vulnerable to open to the flood,

Or hurl against the iron-plated mail

Of their thick sides enormous weight of shot,

Or ponderous shell, screaming and glad for death,

Till both, crushed in their seams by monstrous blows,

Settle and sink sudden into the depths,

And death o'ertakes the crews, and all is still,

The fierce chiefs plied each other with their spears,

And, coming closer, drew their fearful knives
And grappled in a struggle fierce but short,
And fell, close-locked, in death.

     By this the rim
Of western hills, in the cold, wasting light,
Grew indiscriminate ; but up the east
Hung, in gray peaceful depths, the full-orbed moon.
Utterly silent was the field of death.
So then the women, who from far had marked
The waning battle as their heroes fell,
And heard the shouts of triumph and the moans
Of men death-stricken fainter grow and cease,
Warned by the ominous stillness of the eve,
Stole, timid, with all orphaned youths and maids
And infants hushed, as by a ghostly fear,
Across that dreadful field of moon-lit death,
Searching for husbands, brothers, sons.
As when a mother doe, with spotted fawn,
Hides by a runnel in some cool, blue glen,
While the brave stag climbs out on some near hill,
Observant of the huntsman and the hounds,

But, venturing too far, a stealthy shot
Reaches his vitals, and he turns and flies,
Bleeding, and falls before his mate, and dies,
But she and the weak fawn smell o'er his wounds,
And lick his face, and moan, and from their eyes,
Lustrous and large, fall piteous tears, so then,
When all their slain had found and turned them o'er,
And knew the light might never break again
In kindling glances from death-faded eyes,
They sat them down through lingering, painful hours
Of the dim night, and, without utterance, wept.

But when the moon, down her accustomed path
Descending, touched the west, He who o'errules
Particular troubles to the general good,
And pities all, and knows the loyal worth
Of true wives' tears, and tears of children—such
As weep a father slain—He, pitying, sent
A sympathetic shudder through the earth,
And the dead warriors sank to graves of calm.
But all the tears of children and of wives,
In a green hollow of the lonely hills

He gathered in a fountain, that the sun

Dries not in summer heats, but crystal pure

O'erbrims and murmurs through the changing year.

Forever on it flows, that gentle stream,

Fountained by tears, and glides among the hills—

Ne-hawka—in a valley of its own,

And passes happy homes, and smiling farms,

And rolling meadows spotted o'er with flocks

That drink its sweet, cool waters; and so on

Past groves of leafy hickory, and beneath

Low painted bridges, rumbling to a team,

It moves a broadening current, swelled by rains

Or the chill ooze of Spring-dissolving snows,

And mirrors back the splendors of the sun,

And the cold moon, and the wide stream of stars,

Until, at length, it lingers at the marge

Of the untamable Missouri flood,

As loath to mingle its love-hallowed tears

With that fierce, sandy rage; then looks its last

On the sweet heavens by passing day or night,

And sinks beneath the yeasty, boiling waves,

Whose like for might and fury earth has not.

THE RAW HIDE.

THE RAW HIDE.

A certain man, of a small company moving up the great plain of the Platte, in a spirit of bravado, said he would shoot the first Indian he met; which he did, having shortly afterward found a Pawnee woman a little separated from her tribe. But a band of warriors, pursuing, demanded from his companions the surrender of that man; which being refused, the Pawnees made ready to slay the whole company of whites. Whereupon the offender being given into their hands, they flayed him alive. From this circumstance the little stream, on whose banks it occurred, takes the name of the Raw Hide.

I.

I WILL go to the meadows ere sunset,

And gather a wreath for my head ;

I will pluck purple flox and white grass-flowers,

And roses both yellow and red,

And will wreathe me a garland outvying

The splendor of jewels and pearls,

That gleam on the sumptuous foreheads

And bosoms of pale-facéd girls.

And Korux will come in the evening,

And lead me forth under the moon ;

Will see me bedecked for his coming,

And, glad for my simple boon,

Will clasp me, and kiss me, and praise me,

In honest true-lover's way ;

Will tear himself from me sadly,

And—hurry the wedding-day.

O sun, pass on to thy setting :
Be swift to thy golden rest :
Far dearer the tender moonlight,
And the star-beams, that invest
With delicate dreamy glory,
And soft, enraptured grace,
The forms of maid and lover,
And the passion of each face.

O sun, pass on to thy setting,
And bring my Korux here ;
And hasten, O silver moonrise,
And let thy light be clear.
Shine, shine upon my garland,
And flash against my eyes,
That Korux may see the sweetness
Of the heart that in me lies.

Dear, blissful world of blessing,
To me there is one thing plain :
The weight of my life's long pleasure
O'erpasses possible pain.

I cannot believe in trouble,
It lasts but a little hour ;
And its use is only to heighten
Our joy to its utmost power.

A wife with a brave like Korux
To guard her from want and blame
With as gentle a heart as his is—
That glows with so steady a flame,
Will never go sighing, sighing,
For a better world than this,
But will have whatever is needful,
To give her contentment and bliss.

And I shall love him completely—
So worthy is he of love ;
His wishes shall be my study
All other things above ;
For I deem 'twas a passing marvel
That I—such a foolish child—
Should have moved the love of Korux,
On whom all the maidens smiled.

I wonder he passed by Bucks-kau-re,

So slender, and graceful, and tall ;

Or mild-eyed, affectionate Kitick,

The daintiest damsel of all.

What was there in me to allure him,

And win him past maidens like these ?

'Tis hard to determine.   I'm thinking

That Korux was easy to please.

For I am too pale for a beauty—

Too slender, I fear, in the face ;

And sometimes I seem, in my movements,

To lack the true manner of grace.

But yet, I've a heart for my Korux,

Than which not a heart is so true ;

And the hope and the trust that he treasures

With me, he never shall rue.

When he goes out the foremost to battle,

Rejoicing in manhood and might,

I will deck him with plumes and colors,

And make his heart happy and light.

And when he comes back victorious,
Or wounded in sore defeat,
I will exult in my warrior,
And make his welcoming sweet.

True wife shall he ever find me,
And ever at his side :
Wherever he leads I will follow,
Be it over the world so wide.
Closer and closer forever
Shall my life with his intertwine,
As, firm on the oak and its branches,
Fastens the parasite vine.

And now I will go ere the sunset,
And gather a garland of flowers ;
I will wander along by the streamlet,
Where the water-fowl have their bowers
Under reeds and willows and grasses,
And where the wild roses grow ;
And I'll gather and weave in my garland
All the beautiful flowers I know.

And hasten, O happy evening,

And bring the silent moon !

Come, come, O silvery moonrise,

And Korux will come soon.

Shine, shine upon my garland ;

Flow round me, mellow beams,

Till I surpass the ideal

Of my lover's bright day-dreams.

II.

It was a Pawnee maiden,

And down a runnel's bank she went,

Low-murmuring, in her happy heart,

    Her artless, sweet content.

The dwellings of her tribe were near

    The prairies, bright and lone ;

Mild on her face the low sun beamed,

    And fear, it was unknown.

The loveliest maiden she of all,

Where many a dark-eyed maid was fair ;

And on her brow was innocence,

And in her heart no snare.
Her thoughts were all of prosperous love,
    For such alone she knew,
And quiet pictures of long bliss
    Her gentle fancy drew.
The daintiest blooms she sought and culled,
And in a garland deftly bound;
And many a rose and pale grass-flower
Fastened her lovely zone around;
Till, as the sun drooped on the hills,
And slant his rays bedimmed the land,
The maiden viewed her work with joy,
And stayed her cunning hand.
But, homeward ere her steps she turned
And sought the village, that from far
In the low, hazy sunset burned
    Like some red evening star,
She paused a moment by the rill,
To note a slow and rumbling train
Of sutler carles and muleteers
    Come winding o'er the plain.

    3

And much she wondered in her mind
That pale-faced men so toiled for gold,
And braved the summer's fiery heats,
    The winter's bitterest cold,
And left behind them mournful homes,
And tried the hate of hostile lands,
When fish and game were plentiful,
And corn grew with small use of hands.
" Not thus will Korux go from me,"
    The simple maiden thought;
" Content with what supplies our needs,
What else in reason shall be sought ? "

III.

And now, the train, approaching,
Wound up the grass-hedged pleasant road,
With crack of whip, and many an oath
Upon the brutes bestowed.
Full of rough daring were the men
Who ventured through the wilderness ;
For danger they had little care ;

For forms of right some cared still less.

Gain was the principle of most ;

Love of adventure moved them all ;

And fearful must have been that thing

Could those stout hearts appal.

They gathered there from many lands,

And brought the passion of all climes,

And filled the Indian's heart with hate,

And made his wives corrupt betimes,

And choked up avenues of good,

Accessible in simple souls,

To whom the action, not the creed,

Proclaims the element that controls.

Deeds infamous and terrible,

   Through long, long years were done.

Even with the little company

   The maiden viewed, was one

Who o'er his cups in wayside ranch

   Had laid a braggart bet,

With boon companions, he would slay

The Indian first they met.
And now as in the lingering light
The maiden fixed his eye,
Far from the dwellings of her tribe,
And decked with prairie finery,
He laughed a devilish laugh and low,
And thought how opportune it proved,
That one lone, helpless maid was thus
Far from all friendly eyes removed.
The bet was won.   The streamlet's bank
The heavy wagons drew anear,
And all beheld the young girl stand
Quietly looking, without fear ;
And heard a shot, and saw her fall,
Nor paused upon their westward way,
But journeyed on for many an hour
By moonlight calm and gray.

                    IV.

Dear are pure dreams of love to God,
And dear to Him all gentle souls.

The lives of virgin maids He shapes,

And each event therein controls, '

Through trying forms of changing fate,

Through pleasure and through pain ;

Gives length of days, or useful death,

As love and pity should ordain.

A sparrow falls: He, careful, sees ;

A maiden dies, and knows not why ;

And reckless time goes whirling on,

And sport and cruelty go by

With wanton jest and stealthy tread,

As if a crime might be secure.

But He, observant, looks from heaven

   And sends a vengeance sure.

A child that, angling in the rill,

   Concealed 'mid reeds and grass,

Had seen the victim fall, and seen

   The train unheeding pass,

Ran to the village with all speed,

   And told the woful tale ;

And warriors banded in hot haste,

And women trembled and turned pale.

Erelong, in silence, up the plain

A host pursuing passed,

Nor gale-driv'n shadows 'neath the moon

Fly stealthier, or more fast.

And ere the sun above the hills

Had flung his golden banner out,

The sutler company were waked

From stolid slumber by the shout

Of frightened sentries, who were 'ware

That dense, dark masses drew anear

From every side, whose coming thus

    There was good room to fear.

Up from their blankets sprang the carles;

The tethered mules, led in, were tied

Within the circle of the wains

    That now defence supplied.

Each man behind his level gun

Was perched among his bales, or lay

Full-length, deep-hidden in the grass,

    And ready for the fray.

It was a game where one was matched

'Gainst twenty of the fearful foe,

And all the carles might well have been

   Extinguished at a blow ;

But savage folk, more generous far

Than they who wrong them day by day,

Who drive them from their homes, and steal,

   In trade, their goods away,

Have ever shown a keener sense

Of simple justice and good will

Than well-trained men whose minds and hearts

   Historic ages fill.

The Pawnee host round the correll

   Formed an unbroken line ;

Then, quietly, all sat them down

   Till the clear sun should shine,

Lest, in the darkness, there should be

Unwished-for deeds of horror done,

And some with hands uncrimsoned meet

The punishment of the guilty one.

At length the hour befit the deed.

Then three tall chiefs approached
The trembling company at bay,
   And thus their errand broached :
" O men that journey through our land,
   And trespass on our right,
We did not stop you as you passed
   Our village but last night.
We saw your mules and merchandise ;
   We knew you were our foe ;
But you had wives and babes behind,
   And so we let you go.
But you, who boast of better ways,
   You had no heed of us ;
You slew a maiden of our tribe,
   And we forbearing thus.
You shot her as she were a beast,
Nor stopped a moment on your way
To mitigate her dying pains,
And smooth the turf whereon she lay.
So, should we slay you all this morn,
We think we should not do a wrong :

But better it perchance may be
   To suffer much and long,
Ere pushed to furious revenge.
   But this we do demand :
Give up to us the murderer
   With blood upon his hand,
To deal with as seems right to us !
Then go in honest peace your way,
And, as you value our good will,
Keep the remembrance of this day."

V.

In idle parley passed an hour—
An hour it was of reasoning,
And vicious threats on either side—
And much the sutlers strove to bring
Their comrade through his perilous strait.
But fear the Indian did not know :
Vain the appeal to future strife
And deep revenge ; and vain the thought
To pay with gold a price for life.

   3*

At length the warrior bent his bow,
Or raised his flint-lock to his eye,
Impatient with the stubborn carles,
And thinking best that all should die
Where justice had no advocate.
And then the men were fain to yield,
And gave the murderer to his fate,
And so the breach was healed.

But him—the unhappy man of blood—
The avengers hurried to that spot
Where, in last sunset's waning light,
He had the maiden shot.
And there, with cruel taunt and gibe,
    They flayed him that he died,
And left his body to the birds,
    Close by the runnel side ;
But stuffed his skin, and set it up
    Before all evil men,
To warn them, lest so foul a thing
    Should e'er be done again.

And long that pallid monument
Faced sun and rain, and winds that blew ;
And whether it crumbled into dust,
Or what its fate, I never knew.
But the dull stream that winds along,
Low under summer suns, or sweeps
Almost a queenly river when
Snows melt, or heaven unlocks the keeps
Wherein are treasured all the rain,
Takes name from what its banks beside
Long years ago was foully done,
And all men call it the Raw Hide

VI.

The summer is here, and the sunshine ;
The prairie is sprinkled with flowers ;
The winds through the long grasses murmur,
The clouds ripple down in bright showers ;
And the birds and the bees are a-singing ;
The youth fly their steeds o'er the plains ;
And lovers for shy nooks are hunting,
And everywhere happiness reigns.

Ah, no ! I am sick for the maiden
That wandered here late by my side :
I see not the birds and the sunshine,
I heed not the winds as they glide.
I think of the past and the future,
And my eyes are beclouded with tears.
The past is a dream that is vanished ;
The future—what has it that cheers ?

Here, under this mound, she is lying,
To moulder in silence alone ;
She knows not I'm standing above her :
I call, but she heeds not the tone.
Oh, lately she came, if I named her ;
On all that I uttered, she hung ;
And, close as the vine to the oak-tree,
Her spirit to mine ever clung.

She lies in a prison of sorrow ;
The light never breaks on her eyes ;
Her hands are clasped over a bosom
No more to be rounded by sighs.

In darkness, of friendship forgotten,
Unheeding, she slumbers alway.
Ah, soon the form that was fairest
Must be as the formless clay.

The ages shall linger above her
And still shine the pitiless sun ;
The moon shall be tender and dreamy,
The feet of the light winds shall run,
And lovers and maids shall be gathered
In happy and endless embrace ;
But for her, in the ranks of the happy,
Shall never be any more place.

And yet, I am told that a spirit
Was dwelling within her pure frame,
That has gone to a beautiful region,
In a country that no man can name.
A spirit thin, pallid, but lovely,
With eyes that are mistless and bright,
And clad in a robe than the grass-flowers
More perfectly spotless and white.

If so, sweet spirit, await me!

One day I shall come to thy place;

I shall seek thee all over that country,

And yearn for thy loving embrace.

Forget me not, spirit most perfect!

Let Korux remain in thy heart:

Again we will wander together,

Nor one from the other depart.

Where the light never dies in the valleys,

Where the winds never angrily blow,

Far away from the dread of the white man,

What happiness may we know!

And the vows now so painfully broken,

Forever and aye we'll repair.

Oh, spirit beloved, be ready!

Oh, wait for and welcome me there!

THE PRAISE OF NEW LANDS

I.

God bless our sturdy native land—

Its prairies broad, its mountains bare,

    Its rough, cold lakes, its rivers grand,

Its pure, invigorating air.

And bless its blue, enfolding seas,

Its forests, springs, and bloomy leas,

And all the powers and influences

That make this land the land it is.

For here are nurtured, here alone,

The tensest muscle, firmest bone ;

The keenest eye, the sternest will,

And largest power for good or ill.

II.

Where huddled Europe breeds her swarms,

    The Few possess the Many's rights.

The Few have homes, and cheer, and forms
   Of health, and eyes that see delights.
The Many toil from day to day,
And earn such pittance as they may;
But scantily fed and clad, and chilled
By hopes forever unfulfilled,
From infancy to manhood's prime,
And down the mellowing, ripening time
Of hallowed age, they dwell with pain,
Nor manhood's guerdon ever gain.
For, let them struggle as they may
To upward win an equal way,
They learn, at last, 'tis vain to try;
That peasants born must peasants die.

III.

I hold 'twere well to teach our heirs,
   If they would shun the peasant's doom,
Would shun his ignorance and cares,
   To live in States where men have room.
Where entail may not bind the land,
Nor privilege defiant stand;

But where a man of heart and mind
At once expansive place may find.
Teach them that cities are the graves
That bury anxious, toil-worn slaves ;
That while the Few there ride at will,
And of all pleasure have their fill,
The Thousands, hither, thither thrown,
Live not in houses of their own—
Scarce know the wind-tone of a tree,
The song-bird's wondrous minstrelsy,
The murmur of a pebbly rill,
And all the sights and sounds that fill
The country with such peace and rest.
Then to the north, or south, or west !
Then to new lands, unless, born great,
One heirs a competent estate !
And be new lands or warm or cold,
Or forest dense, or open wold,
Or inland far, or by the sea,
Thither let poor-folk straightway flee,
And know that who to new lands come,
May own themselves and own their home.

IV.

But ah, to leave forefathers' graves,

　　And sights well-loved from infancy :

Were it not better still be slaves

　　Than all we love no more to see ?

Better to linger by the looms,

Better to pace dark, rented rooms ;

Better to breathe the putrid air

Of dusty, narrow streets and bare ;

Better to meet each coming year

With lessening hope and deepening fear,

That still in sunshine and in shower

Fond eyes may see the old church-tower,

Fond ears still hear the sweet church-bell,

Whose summons blest we love so well—

Still round us move the patient grace

Of many a loved familiar face,

And that, by graves most dear, at last

We may lie down when life is past ?

V.

O weak one, filled with discontent
Of present things, yet fearing change,
Let life have purpose ere 'tis spent—
    Give thought and action broader range !
The wilderness is sweet as wide,
And fair the forms on every side
Of hill and valley, mead and wood—
I would that old lands were as good !
In happy murmurs glide the rills,
And golden splendor falls and fills
The heaven above the fragrant glens ;
Nor wild beast there, nor snaky fens.
Go, deem what prospect most invites :
There rear thy home, and bring the rites
Of prayer and worship : fill a space
With lettered and with mannered grace,
Till church-bells sound from vale to vale,
And gardens on the air exhale
The orient perfume of the rose.
Life shall have purpose as it goes,

And good be done, and strength increase,
And old age win an honored peace.

VI.

For many a year, across these plains,
   I've marked the stalwart immigrant
Guiding his scantly-laden wains
   To some fair nook, anew to plant
The fortunes of his family tree.
And when, erelong, he there might be,
The spacious homestead rose serene,
Embowered in cool, inviting green ;
The lark sang sweetly at his door ;
His barns were filled with ample store ;
His fields all spotted o'er with kine
Indolent in the broad sunshine ;
While on the road his carriage shone,
And far and wide his name was known
As one to whom all men might flee
For certain hospitality :
The stranger's counsel, orphan's friend,

Ready to harbor, help, or lend,

Ready in church and neighborhood,

To do the righteous thing he could.

And, year by year, more perfect grace

Was written in his manly face,

Till every look and action went

To speak his measureless content.

VII.

Men grow by independent thought—

   Self-centred action unconstrained.

Far greater he whose lines are wrought

   By purpose in himself contained,

Than he who by another's will

Some petty place must daily fill—

Some tiresome, endless, dull routine,

That makes him but a mere machine.

Give me a hut with scanty cheer,

Far on the blooming wild frontier—

A yoke of cattle, and a cow,

And acres of my own to plow—

A dog, a gun, the sweet blue skies,

And Nature's charms and mysteries ;—

So I may feel that I am free,

And master of my fortunes be ;—

So I may ride, or sit, or play,

Or read my book each stormy day ;—

So I may see my comforts grow,

With immigration's onward flow ;—

See values rise, and friendship grace

Each neighbor's honest, manly face,—

And I shall feel myself a king,

Compared with them who daily wring

Precarious substance from small wage,

Nor hoard a little for old age.

VIII.

Thank God, new lands are vast as fair :

   Earth for her millions still has room—

Has wealth of plains, and mountain-air,

   And breezy coasts, and forests' gloom,

Where all conditions may find place.

On some fair future day of grace,

Along the regions now but waste,

Civilizations shall be traced

As fair as any that may be.

Then, from his grave, might one but see

His sons and daughters firmly set,

Where wealth and honor purely met—

Might see his race adorn their name,

And bless the ancestor that came

Into the wilds, with sturdy heart

To give his house that prosperous start,

Some joy might stir his palsied breast,

Some sweet contentment fill his rest.

IX.

But, ah ! we cannot raise a theme,

   Or sing a song, or chant a stave,'

Or yield awhile to some bright dream,

   But it must end low in the grave.

We plant; our children take and reap,

But quickly they are laid asleep.

   4

The winds and waters murmur on,

The sun forgets the nations gone,

And to and fro pass heedless feet.

Oh ! much is wanting to complete

The barest possibilities

Would make this life a thing of bliss.

No region may be found on earth

To wholly fit the immortal worth

Of God-given souls whose end is God.

There is no place from Him abroad—

No country where He veils His eyes,

And talks with thunder from the skies,

And sends the slow approach of death—

Where men may draw all-happy breath.

For something still all true souls pant—

Some unrelievable want,

That Heaven alone can satisfy.

Heaven is the country to draw nigh—

The home of the aspiring soul :

There men are sound, and true, and whole,

And lands are fair, and skies are pure,

And homes and friendships that endure.

Towards heaven we tend.   God give us grace

To see, without great fear, His face;

And give us room where all is new

To us poor earth-worms, blind of view,

And foolish in our weak designs.

And, like the sun that months-long shines

Upon the erewhile darkened pole,

Backward death's darkness may He roll,

And set us where no want is known—

Under the splendor of His throne.

NEBRASKA—1866.

THE virgin of the wilderness,
  She sits upon her hills alone;
Loose sprigs of cedar in her hair,
  A vine-wreath round her zone;
As gray-eyed Pallas pure and free,
Expectant of the things to be.

No robe of art in pliant fold
Wraps her deep bosom from the cold,
Nor rustling veil, nor cheap disguise,
Conceals the freshness of her eyes.

Beneath her feet an hundred rills
Flash, singing to the naked hills;
And forest-belted rivers glide
Through prairie valleys, warm and wide.

Not hers are breadths of palm or pine,
Or sands of gold, or mountain mine,

Or dizzy steeps, or barren rocks,
But farm-land vales and grass for flocks ;
   And over her, spanned in splendor, rise
Mild, changeful depths of cheerful skies.

She looks across her vacant lands,
   And feels a virgin's conscious shame ;
Yet not with her to shape the past—
   Oh, not with her the blame !
She smiles benign on every guest,
And proffers shelter, food, and rest.
To empires thronged with men, afar,
To states where discord dwells, and war,
She calls, and shows her ample bound,
And peace within, and peace around.
To families distressed and poor,
To restless sage and o'ertasked boor,
To broken health and courage spent,
To all the sons of discontent,
Where'er they pine, whate'er they be,
She cries, " Be thine a homestead free—

A lordly right of wealthy land,

And health, ease, quiet.   At my hand

   Receive the cool, sustaining hours,

And energize thy weakened powers."

She knows that she was born to be

   The mother of a mighty race :

Heroic sons whom reverence seeks—

   Daughters to wear all grace ;—

That on her soil there yet must rise

Whatever prospects good men prize :

The pure church, up whose heaven-topped spire

Creeps the long sunset's lingering fire ;

The college in whose reverend shade

Unpolished youths are Grecians made ;

And tasteful homes ; and those calm keeps

Where musing memory broods and weeps.

She knows, elate, that she was born

To blend the sunset with the morn ;

To add new vigor to the chain

That links the mountain to the main ;

Till, growing greater and more great,

She sits the peer of every state;

And all shall love and call her blest—

The virgin Mother of the West.

THE MISSOURI.

I.

Who shall sing the song of the River—

Channel of Empire, Highway of God,

That from the depths under far northern mountains—

Sunless and cold as the caves of the sea—

Riseth Titanic, grand monarch of Rivers?

Strong in its birth, every league it grows stronger;

Cleaveth the land into wide, blooming valleys;

Parteth asunder the hills from each other;

Mineth the forest to drift it away,

Or fix, like a spear in couch for a tilt,

The huge woodland monarch, a desperate sawyer,

To vex the thin keels on the pathway of commerce.

II.

Restless forever and shifting its current—

Emblem of Time and the progress of nations—

4*

See how it rushes, resistless, unsparing,

Onward, right onward, rejoicing in might !

Tawny and rough as an old crouching lion,

Hark ! how it roars through the valleys afar !

Trust not its temper ; 'tis best at betraying :

Never it sports but in anger and fury.

Sternly in earnest, unstaying in purpose,

Forward it sweeps to the Gulf of the Tropics.

Not by its islands a moment delays it ;

Not by the shadows that lurk by the shore ;

Straight as an arrow that flies to its target,

Hastes it right on, as 'twere bent upon Duty.

Hastes ! and no dimple or low-rippling laughter

Answers, seductive, the bright glance of noon,

But always volcanic, it bursts in fierce eddies,

And tumbles and surges in long-heaving billows,

And crumbles and buries the banks that would hold it.

III.

Master it is of the broad Mississippi—

Paramount lord of that good-natured flood !

Grasps the strong affluent as athlete, or savage ;

Fixes, exultant, its serf-mark of service—

Dark, dirty-yellow, the sands of the uplands.

Thence to the Gulf descending, it welters

Through the fat bottoms that lie to the Sun

Fervid as Danæ to love-freighted gold-showers,

And as black Egypt propitiously fruitful.　.

In its deep bosom, far out to the Delta

Bears it the soils of the lands there uprising—

Lands to be covered by numerous people

Fast as the sea recedes, or the earthquake

Heaves the low bars into long, level stretches—

Tame to the eye, but surpassingly fertile.

IV.

Type of my country, the mighty, the chainless,

Heir of the best and the worst in all ages—

Splendor and turbulent license of Greece—

Roll on forever, majestic, unshackled,

Reaching afar, through the hills and the prairies,

Thy bountiful arms, the bonds of our Union !

Bear to the ocean the wealth of a region

Vaster, and richer by nature, than Europe ;

Pour through the land beneficent commerce—

Parent of art that is lovely and lasting ;

Bind in firm concord the states once dissevered ;

Untangle base interests—the interests conflicting,

Till from the Delta afar to thy fountains

One patriot mind is wholly pervasive.

But, should this people be prone to rebellion,

Heedless of freedom, honor, and right,

Rise up from thy channel in terror a deluge ;

O'erwhelm the broad fields, the opulent cities ;

Destroy the promoters of public disaster,

And roll on in gloom, vast, mournful, and shoreless,

God only beholding, the Judge and Avenger.

1865.

GRAPING.

Down by the dull Cahokia,
   Just back from a sandy shore,
You and I went a-graping,
   In the pleasant days of yore.
We sat in the glancing shadows,
   Or roamed in the open sun ;
But of grapes—alas ! my darling—
   We fetched not a single one.

Our baskets came back empty,
   But our hearts were full of dreams,
Inwrought with the warm October
   And the sunset's mellow beams.
O sweet through the fading grasses
   Wandered the wind's low moan,
And, piping their cheerful signals,
   Went birds to a summer zone.

Your hand in my own was resting,
  But few were the words we spoke ;
And our pitiless companions
  Shot at us many a joke.
But little we cared, my darling ;
  We had plighted our secret truth,
And the world seemed a purple vine-land,
  Hung full for the wants of youth.

Then, ere the leaves had fallen,
  Or cold blew the northern gale—
Ere the sun swam low in the tropics,
  Or the skies were chilly and pale,
The villagers all came trooping—
  The greatest as well as the least—
To hear our vow's confession
  Before the surpliced priest.

And out through Autumn's glories,
  Or ever the day was done,
We had crossed broad river and prairie,
  In the track of the hazy sun.

And the still night closed around us,

    And Dian smiled bright above

Our shrine of the perfumed Hymen,

    And the sacrifice of love.

Oh, swift the years as the passage

    Of pigeons with silvery wings;

And deep in their silence is hidden

    All tender and holy things—

The smiles, the kisses, the rapture,

    The sighs, the unsealing of tears,

The darkness that fills with amazement,

    The light in the west that cheers.

They are full of children's voices,

    And songs by the cradle sung;

Of the shadowy gleam of faces—

    Forever fair and young—

That paled in their opening promise,

    And under the willows hide.

Ah, Heaven seems far less distant

    Since the little ones have died!

And once again we are graping,

    But not near the dear old home ;

New lands are ever unstable—

    Their people like Arabs roam.

We follow our children westward ;

    They will follow theirs to the sea.

Few men in the land are settled,

    Or know where their graves shall be.

I like, in the mild October,

    These rides in the country air,

The plats 'neath the swaying woodlands,

    And the sunlight flickering there.

I love the merry laughter

    Of the groups at the clustered vine, .

And the glimpse of faces rosy

    As Moenads flushed with wine.

For, like a wind that freshens

    One drooping and moving slow,

These things throw over my spirit

    The spell of the long-ago ;

And I'm proud that these young people,
    Like those of our youthful days,
Have pleasure in simple pleasures,
    And love the old-fashioned ways.

But, for us, the scramble is ended,
    'Tis time to be sober and still;
We are nearing the mist-covered river—
    Are down at the foot of the hill.
Our baskets have ever been empty—
    A trifle our slender store;
Yet only for you and the children
    Have I ever wished for more.

I hope, when the final summons
    Is sped from the ghostly king,
Afar to a peaceful country
    Together our souls may wing;—
Together may live in glory,
    And round us the children play,
As once in the long-gone summers,
    Ere some were taken away.

But now, my arm for the wagon!

　The horses are placed abreast,

For the home-bound sun is nearing

　His gate in the golden west:

And the wind, with murmur tender,

　Dies out in a long, long sigh;

And the bird to his mate is calling

　That the chill, dark night is nigh.

THE DEATH OF THE STAG.

THE skies are bright with dewy light;
   The gray old peaks are softly glowing;
The hunter's horn rings on the height,
And the timid deer, in wild affright,
Leaps down the valley, where shades of night
   Under rivers of mist are flowing.

Away below the fleet hounds go,
   Their music like far clarions ringing;
Away under tree-boughs pendant low,
Across dim meadows, glimmering slow
To a hazy dawn, and by curve and flow
   Of a stream in its rock-bed singing.

Now there, now here—now faint, now clear,
   The echoes of the hunt are flying.
Too quiet seems this atmosphere
For a skurrying chase of sport and fear;

But oh ! a ringing shot and cheer,
  And the stag is down and dying.

A moment dim the bright hills swim
  Past eyes that gaze with weak endeavor ;
Then darkness fills their azure rim—
The tepid airs blow chill for him—
A shudder glances from limb to limb—
  And his flights are done forever.

But sweet its note, from rhythmic throat,
  The hunter's horn is gayly flying ;
It sails through glens, o'er peaks remote,
Its silvery echoes backward float
Soft as Pan's pipe, or pastoral oat,
  Or the west wind's dreamy sighing.

TO THE SOUTH WIND.

Oh, blandly blow,

South Wind, and flow

Along these barren fields of snow,

Till melt their flakes,

And winter takes

His homeward flight past frontier lakes.

Disperse his chills !

Release the rills,

To swirl and ripple through the hills !

Call star-eyed flowers

To deck the bowers,

Through which shall dance the twinkling Hours.

Waft feathery droves

To fill our groves

With nymphic songs and fruitful loves !

From vales and rocks

Let bleating flocks

Respond afar to crowing cocks !

Bring odorous balm

From lands of palm,

To steep my soul in tropic calm ;

Subdue each sense

O'erwrought, intense,

To stillness and to indolence !

Then let me lie

Where tall pines sigh,

And listen as thou murmurest by,

Or 'neath broad vine

Watch shade and shine

Flutter, pursue, and intertwine,

Like human fates

That mystery mates

In troubled flow through life's estates—

A clouded dance,

A swift advance

Through trying changes of mischance.

Dear, mellow chime

Of summer time!

Blest voice of that entrancing clime

Where never beat

The angry feet

Of icy winds and Titan sleet,

Along these dells,

Like distant bells

Be heard again thy joyous swells—

Thy flute-note calls,

Thy breath that falls

An echo from heaven's crystal walls,

Luring afar

From moil and jar,

To heights where purple dream-lands are;

Fore-running peace

And fat increase,

And all that gives our want release.

Prophet of wealth

And jocund health—

Doer of charities by stealth,

The sick e'er bless

Thy soft caress,

And grateful smile, and suffer less.

Young children's feet

Through fields and street

Bound playful forth thy play to meet;

And fond youths vie,

'Neath moon-lit sky,

Which best may shine in Beauty's eye.

Sitting at ease,

The old man sees

Thy billowy sporting on the leas,

Till, with like roll,

Beyond control,

The past flows backward through his soul.

Thy gentle airs,

Beguiling cares,

Draw pure souls upward unawares;

Through willowy wave
Thy lonely stave
Sighs, like a mourner, o'er the grave.

No tyrant thou,
With iron brow
And force to bend—no matter how!
No blustering knave
To roar and rave,
And prove to worms that thou art brave!

Heaven's blessed child,
Low-voiced and mild,
Thou teachest men ambition-wild,
That who do most
At duty's post,
Ask notice least, make least of boast;

And courteous move,
Intent to prove
The wise omnipotence of love;

5

Their faith their cheer—

And bright and clear

Their names shall at the last appear.

So, South Wind, blow,

And cheerily flow

Along these barren fields of snow:

Flow like sweet rhymes;

Bring happier times,

Dear angel of celestial climes!

RALLYING SONG—1864

Up, Freemen of the Northland—
  Up, for your country calls!
The foe hovers near your border—
  His foot on the Fatherland falls.
Is this an hour for wrangling?
  It is crime to bandy words.
Go, harness your steeds for the battle!
  Flash forth your unpitying swords!
    Clang the bells, and toll them!
    Rattle the drums, and roll them!
    Wave the banners, and lustily shout
To the laggards at home, "Turn out! Turn out!"

Stand forth, as your sires before you,
  Close-ranked in dreadful might!
And hurry away to the conflict—

Your war-cry, " God and the right ! "
Must the nation fall ?   Let its crash
  Be unheard for your widows' crying ;
Let it sink to the booming of cannon,
  And die in the groans of the dying.
      Mantle your bells, and toll them !
      Muffle your drums, and roll them !
      While earth lays bare her motherly breast,
And gathers her heroes to gory rest.

THE UNKNOWN SAIL AT NANTUCKET.

FROM out the indeterminable distance
  There comes a sail
That, moving landward—urged by joint persistence
  Of tide and gale—

Flies o'er the tract of intervening ocean,
  A stately thing,
As floats a hawk in heaven without a motion
  Of plume or wing.

And while we wait to learn her name and story,
  And what prevails—
Or haply pleasure, gain, or dream of glory,
  To lift her sails,

She shifts her course, and, gliding past our island,
    Is swift withdrawn,
Till her dim topsail looms like some far highland,
    And then is gone.

But the gray billows, with unceasing motion
    And utterance lone,
From the deep bosom of the ancient ocean
    Give back a moan

That bodies forth a sense of separation
    None may elude,
The long monotony and expiration
    Of solitude.

Thus, on the highways marked by play or duty,
    We come and go,
And past us eyes that speak, and forms of beauty,
    Glide to and fro.

But, while we turn to reach a hand, or utter
    Some word of grace,
They swiftly pass and leave, with just a flutter,
    An empty space.

Vainly we cry, " Who are these ? "   " Whence depart-
  ing ? "
          And " Whence were they ? "
Just this is clear : across our pathway starting,
          They speed away.

And be their lives attractive as their presence,
          Or flushed with shame ;
And be their homes with sorrow or with pleasance,
          'Tis all the same.

They are to us henceforth as memories only
          That dimmer grow—
As songs that sink to echoes faint and lonely,
          Then cease to flow.

Or as the ship that with majestic motion
          Drew near the shore,
And made no port ; but the cold, restless ocean
          Moaned as before.

FAIR AND FRAIL.

" Fair and Frail ! " the people say ;
   " Fair and Frail—a child of sin ! "
Manhood, jibing, turns away ;
   Matrons will not let her in.

Not a friend in all the world !
   Whence she comes, and whither goes,
By life's tempests whipped and whirled,
   Not a blameless Christian knows.

Must she pillow in the street ?
   Tender child, the nights are cold !
Doubtless some will guide her feet
   To the harlot's ghastly fold.

Where, I wonder, was her home ?
   Where are father's, mother's care ?
   5*

From their harshness did she roam
    Forth to meet the ready snare?

See, a shadow fills her eyes,
    And her face is wan with thought!
Does she blame the holy skies
    For the hardness of her lot?

Does she breathe a weary prayer
    Sometimes in her sinful breast—
Wishful of Christ's pitying care,
    Wishful of His sovereign rest?

She is human—what are we?
    Who may hope, unless forgiven,
E'er a better life to see,
    E'er to gain a perfect heaven?

Man awards her scorn for wrong;
    Matrons fear her wicked ways:
Peaceful homes to these belong—
    Hers are sinful nights and days.

Why, good people, hold her vile,
    Wink, and whisper low her name,

When you flatter, fawn, and smile
  On, the wretch who wrought her shame ?

Have you thought who cursed her so ?—
  Dragged her down from innocence ?—
Sought her love to work her woe ?—
  Fooled her by a vain pretence ?

Seek, unmask him, cast him forth !
  Let him feel how foul his wrong !
Place him by his proper worth—
  Devils not with men belong !

But for her—hope's trusting child—
  Christians, open hand and heart !
Fear not you to be defiled,
  When you act your Master's part ! ,

He who once with sinners kept,
  And from none His love withdrew,
E'en for her He prayed and wept,
  And would save her. But would you ?

THE FORGOTTEN POET.

'Tis a ballad from Percy's Reliques,
    Written hundreds of years ago ;
But the head that planned, and the hand that wrote,
    Forgotten, in dust are low.

The song goes on with the ages,
    And earns well-merited fame ;
But no one asks where the Singer lies dead,
    Or seeks to revive his name.

Yet sweet must have been the spirit
    Could make a song that will live ;
From stores more ample than he can impart,
    Each gives what he has to give.

But little, perchance, it matters,
    When any thing noble is done,
That men, admiring, shall speak in praise,
    Or a wreath of bays be won.

And one who has ended his mission,
    And gone to an honored sleep,
Oh, what can he care for an empty name,
    That struggles a place to keep?

Enough it is for the Singer
    That his song has been well sung;
That it lingers to lighten the sorrowful heart,
    Or trips on the cheerful tongue.

Enough it is for the Singer
    That God, whose Singer he is,
Has given him vision, and strength of speech,
    And filled him with melodies;

And taken him up some higher,
    Where the Singers' harps are gold;
Where the singing is never ended, and where
    There is no one forgotten or old.

TO ZEPHYR.

Dance to me, sing to me;
Swift Sweet, and fling to me
Kisses more soft than the leaf of the rose;
Ripple, and wing to me;
Speed, speed, and bring to me
Secrets too dainty for words to disclose.

Fondly, O glide to me;
Arms open wide to me;
Pour round my being thy rapturous grace;
Lean on, confide to me;—
What! art denied to me?
Sweet, I am faint for the breath of thy face.

Zephyr, come nigh to me;
Lisp to me, sigh to me;

Tell me thy passion; 'twill lighten thy heart.

Vain is my cry to thee;

Still wilt go by to me?

Well, then, I scorn thee!   Poor trifler, depart

MISTHER O'FLANAGAN'S ADVOISE TIL A CUNTHRYMAN.

On, cum til Ameriky, Paddy,

    No matther how good yer istate is;

'Tis a land wid a tech uv the carn-joos,

    The chisest uv cabbige and 'taties.

A shanty here rints for jist nothin',

    Or a cellar that's nice for a laddy;

An' the pigs runs roun' loose in the night-time,

    Gruntin', " Ate me, an' thanks til ye, Paddy."

As for biznis, 'tis plinty an' aisy;

    Ye kin live like a prince or a Turruk;—

Unless they bring in thim low Chinese,

    There'll allus be plinty of wurruk.

There's railroads forever is bildin',

    An' conthracts is given away—

Jobs fatther than iver ye dhramed uv,

    That clare ye two dollars a day.

Yere a vother as soon as ye cum here—
  Invited to parties and balls;
An' they sind ye right aff til the Congriss—
  An' the jails all has tumble-down walls.
Ye kin do as ye plase, an', be jabers,
  There's nothin' on airth to be fearin';
Ivry sowl here igspicts to git office,
  An' smiles to the igziles uv Erin.

May the Vargin look swate to ould Ireland,
  An' dhrive from it Inglish an' ill:
I've taken an oath uv alleginse,
  But I am an Oirishman still.
An' this is the r'ason I'm lovin'
  An' praisin' this land uv the free;
Ye kin sware iv'ry day to be loyal,
  An' yit a true Fenian be.

So cum til Ameriky, Paddy;
  Bring Biddy, an' all uv the brats!
Giv' yer lan'lord a taste uv shillalah—
  Turn over yer hovel to rats!

Bring Biddy, the jewil—och, bliss her !—

    Hir ize like a diamon' shine ;

Her breath is as swate as a posy,

    Her lips is as lushus as wine,

LONGING.

The leaf is yellowing on the tree,
   The grass is fading at my feet;
The sad wind murmurs from the sea
Of things that nevermore shall be,
   And cold and slow the wavelets beat.

Far off against the sullen cloud
   A misty sail a moment stands,
Like a pale ghost that in its shroud
One glimpse of mortals is allowed,
   And then must flit to shadowy lands.

Oh, sail far-bound across the sea,
   Would that my fate were linked with thine;—
That brighter skies these eyes might see,
And bloom-clad shores, where misery
   Leaves not on heart or brow a line!

That I might clasp the pallid hands

    Whose loving pressure thrills me yet ;

Might stand beside her where she stands,

And wander with her through fair lands,

    And all my solemn cares forget !

NEBRASKA, DEAR NE-BRASKA!

Nebraska, dear Nebraska!

    Thy hills are far away,

Thy bowery vales, where lingers

    The long-enamored day.

But sweet the scented west-wind,

    As flute-notes o'er the sea,

Ripples from yonder sunset,

    And tells my heart of thee.

What though day's dying glories

    Last crown the mountain lone,

And many a land has prospects

    Far lovelier than thine own?

I roam by mount and river,

    I pass by lake and lea,

To note their mingled beauties,

    Then homeward turn to thee.

And still the sea may thunder
   Far-breaking on the shore,
And still the windy pine-woods
   Send back responsive roar ;
And cool beneath the mountain
   May lie the azure lake,
And down the rocky ledges
   The silvery cataract break.

Far dearer are thy meadows,
   Thy rounded grassy hills,
Thy sandy-bedded rivers,
   Thy shallow, reedy rills.
For not a land is lying
   Beneath the heaven's broad dome,
Can proffer such contentment
   As fills the land of home.

Oh, there's a spot made holy,
   Deep in thy sheltering breast—
A spot of calm seclusion
   Where loved ones are at rest ;

And there, when wanderings over,

    And gone life's little day,

May I with them be lying,

    And mingle clay with clay.

    6

LOTHAIR.

WRITTEN IN MY COPY OF DISRAELI'S LATE NOVEL.

I THANK thee, Premier, in my deepest heart
   For this profound and masterly Lothair !
   'Tis all as it should be, except that Clare
Arundel.   Pity it seems with her to part
So sadly ;—she, the gem of all this art !
   For neither Theodora, Corisande,
   Nor any other lady, sweet, or grand,
Brings so much beauty, passion, to Love's mart,
   As she who wears the Jesuit's slimy coils,
And mars with sable weeds her beauteous youth.
   Thus hath it often been.   I've seen the toils
Of superstition bind some maiden's truth
   On whom men looked desiring : love used foils :
The best went by, moved to regretful ruth.

MAGDALEN.

A BURNING, weary waste of years,
A torture of disease and fears,
And yet, alas ! not many tears :
    The heart must feel ere eyes can fill.
As farther and fainter the strokes be
Of bells on ships that sail to seâ,
So humbled conscience spoke to me
    With lessening voice, and then was still.

Ah, I have known fierce greed and hate,
And pride cold, but importunate,
And lust that never would abate,
    But glowed through pain a fire of hell ;
All passions with a tooth to gnaw,
Crimes, too, that skulk at thought of law,
And leave the body a sapless straw,
    A moving mummy, a soulless shell.

And yet no blood is on my hands ;
No pale ghost ever near me stands,
With eyes that burn like fiery brands,
    My fitful slumbers to affright.
What I have done—well, I have done ;
But deadlier sentence might be won,
And redder currents might have run
    Across these hands so thin and white.

For I have sometimes brooded much
On vengeance ; and have leaped to clutch
A dagger keen and cold to touch,
    With will at point to give the blow.
But force unseen curbed headlong wrath ;
The viper slid across my path,
Nor knew how close for fatal math
    Death followed, vengeful of my woe.

God lets him live.   God's ways are good,
Though not by me well understood.
Why prospers the man ?   My orphanhood—
    Why was it defenceless and defiled ?

I know I once was pure as snow,

My heart as light as winds that blow,

And cheek as tender as morning glow,

    And eyes not fierce as now, but mild.

Then, earth seemed very clean and sweet;

Where things made single moved to meet,

A sure perfection to complete,

    And nights were short, and days were long.

A good man reared me as his own;

By his revered name I was known,

And ever around, like leaves, were strewn

    Comfort and culture, books and song.

Till life moved to a quicker strain;

I loved, and seemed beloved again;

But love grew thorny and full of pain,

    And what was asked, alas! was given.

It was not passion broke my heart;

I thought to act a wifely part,

Nor ever dreamed my lover's art

    Was the fashion of hell and not of heaven;

'Till, when our nuptial hour was set,
The groom came not.   But guests were met,
And many spoke a cold regret,
   And hoped to see me yet a bride.
But long ere dawn that cruel day
The man had fled—none knew what way;
And I, a cast-off thing, must stay,
   Nor find a shelter at his side.

Months rolled along, and with them came
A consciousness that burned like flame
Within my mind.   I knew that shame
   Must henceforth be my hapless lot.
I, too, took wings, and blindly fled:
Whither, I cared not.   Let day shed
No beam upon me.   Count me dead;
   And be my name by all forgot.

My child—thank God!—brief space did see:
I was so full of misery,
Small vital force in him could be.
   He sleeps, a head-stone at his grave;

Wages of shame procured that stone ;

And harlot-fingers there have grown

Sweet flowers, that summer-long have blown,

    And willows that toss like a wandering wave.

Years now I've wandered far and wide,

Restless, and nowhere can abide ;

And once, upon an eventide,

    Far in the west the man I met.

His eye was musing, deep, and cold—

A moment held, then sidewise rolled.

I doubt if he knew me, I'm grown so old ;

    But he seems young as ever yet.

I found his home when darkness came—

A home well worthy of the name,

Since not for him, as me, was shame ;—

    His sin concealing he passed for wise.

There, through a shutter, streaming bright,

Flamed forth upon the moonless night

The peaceful glory of a light,

    And set a picture to my eyes :

      6*

A fond, young wife as sweetly fair
As any creature of the air ;
And, smiling, innocent of care—
   Her sky of happiness unflecked ;—
Smiling on him who did me wrong,
As, with a gentle arm and strong,
He danced his boy to merry song,
   Nor my near presence did suspect.

The boy, he wore his father's face—
The same bold carriage, yet with grace,
That to his mother I could trace—
   And how could I but hate that child ?
I thought upon a far-off grave—
A child that never pleasure gave—
A child no father sought to save—
   On whom its mother never smiled.

And who was she who sat that night
Within the warm and lovely light,
In womanhood complete and white,
   So happy with him I should have loved ?

Why stood I in the frosty gloom,
Foul as a creature of the tomb,
And saw another in the room
    From whence, to this, I was removed?

My guardian taught me, " God is just; "
Believe it I am sure I must,
Since things unknown we take on trust;
    But justice sometimes lingers long.
I thought, for many days, to be
The avenger of my misery,
And give that man what he gave me—
    The hell, to which we both belong.

But, as I hid from night to night,
Some spell my purpose seemed to blight;
Some thought my weak heart would affright,
    Till to red vengeance I grew loth.
Let him enjoy what fate endears;
Let no want blight his infants' years;
His wife's sweet eyes be free of tears;
    Alone I suffer enough for both.

So, like a wolf, I slipped away,

And they—are happy, I dare say ;

But I—I live as best I may,

   And kill the time that moves too slow.

Sometimes I'm here, sometimes I'm there ;

But ever at a fight with care,

And ever striving to look fair ;

   And life is short, I'm glad to know.

For no man looks with sympathy,

Or ever speaks true words to me :

Yet do I have much flattery

   And looks that sometimes pass for love.

But sneers may follow the softest sigh ;

And, passion glutted, the melting eye

Seeks other faces as I go by,

   Or studies the street, or roofs above.

So let it be.   While sands may run,

I shall be outcast and undone—

The wife of many, not of one—

   A thing few pity, and all blame.

Fair dames, I beg you, hurry fast;

And, gentles, ah, as you go past,

Let virtuous, stony looks be cast

    On her you fee for hours of shame!

I'm so accustomed to all scorn,

Nothing can make me more forlorn,

Except it be that I adorn

    A body daily growing old.

Oh, much I doubt, when beauty's gone,

And I am haggard, weak, and wan,

If fish may in my net be drawn—

    If I may cope with want and cold.

Perchance, when time shall come to weep,

It may be best to go to sleep:

I know a stream that's swift and deep,

    Not far away from a child's grave.

If there I perish, who will care?

What face a saddened look will wear?

The world has many like me to spare—

    Too many for each a tear to crave.

I sometimes wish a virtuous soul,

With boundless lucre at control,

Might greatly want to see me whole,

    Almost as once, ere days of shame:

Might give of means he cannot need,

And rear a home to house and feed

Us hardened wretches, and would plead

    There with us in his Master's name.

But this is idle—painful, too.

He who seeks me will come to woo :

Inside the door you'll find his shoe,

    When darkness veils the stealthy street.

Would he might come while yet 'tis day,

And bear this suffering frame away,

To moulder in the friendly clay !

    And what is future, let me meet.

RELIGIOUS POEMS.

ASPIRATION.

On, to be holy, as Jesus is holy !
  Oh, to be pure, as my Saviour is pure !
Growing, through patience, more humble, more lowly ;
  Learning, in meekness, to toil and endure !

Patient, through trial, to love and to duty ;
  Cheerfully bearing life's losses and pain ;
Looking above for fruition of beauty ;
  Faithful in service before I would reign !

Never to doubt, since my dear Lord before me
  Trod the rough path over which I must go ;
Never to fear if the thunder boom o'er me,
  Or if a gale from Gethsemane blow.

But as a city that shines o'er the valleys,
  Beacon to pilgrims perplexed by the way,

True to my Leader wherever He rallies,
  Of His full brightness reflecting some ray ;

Let me remain, till the Day of Thanksgiving
  Dawn in the white of eternity drest ;
Uprightly, blamelessly, manfully living,
  Then peacefully dying ;—with God be the rest.

1865.

SAD HEART, SOW IN TEARS.

Sad heart, sow in tears :
   Gain not to keep !
God tills by heart-aches
   Many and deep.
Trust and believe Him ;
   Soon you shall reap.

Into the furrow
   Falls the bright grain ;
Clouds gather over it,
   Beats the wild rain.
When comes the harvest,
   Great is the gain.

Sad heart, sow in tears
   Gain not to keep !

C

Fierce if the trial,
    Sweet is the sleep.
Rest for the weary—
    Ah, it is deep.

IT MATTERS NOT.

It matters not—it matters not
   How little anxious toil can give,
Or how obscure the unyielding lot
   Through which we move and live.
If hearts grow gentle, pure, and wise,
Deriving from above supplies
To guide the will and energies,
   What else may be—it matters not.

It matters not—it matters not
   If friends be false or friends be true,
Or what the world may wish or wot,
   Or if it give our due.
Each soul within itself contains
A separate destiny, whose gains
Are some of peace, but more of pains:
   So let all be—it matters not.

It matters not—it matters not

    If times wax worse as they advance ;

If fiercer grows the war of thought,

    And lewder song and dance.

Reforms reach but the single mind ;

No law of right the mass can bind ;

A jewel here and there we find :

    What others are—it matters not.

It matters not—it matters not

    If measured sands are wasting fast ;

If soon must come a day unsought—

    That day, for us, the last.

Since all that moves desire or pride

Into oblivion must subside ;

Eternity, quick open wide—

    And time's poor dream—it matters not.

CHRISTMAS EVE—1869.

Come, sing the angels' song to-night!
That song forever sweet, as when
First broke from out the starry height
"Glory to God, good-will to men."
And sing as love prolongs the strain
The Mother mild, the wondrous birth
Of Him who plucked the thorn from pain,
And left His peace with sinful earth.

Long past His sufferings and toil—
The bloody death, the gloomy grave—
The homeward triumph from the spoil
Of foes too fierce for men to brave.
He sits, to-night, the King of Kings,
Enthroned above the throngs of light,
Who hide their faces with their wings,
And chant His glory, grace, and might.

The ages draw their lingering length—
    Their flying change of sun and shade;
And hate moves nations by its strength,
    And weakness is of power afraid.
Yet not reversed our God's decree
    Foreshadowed in the angels' song,
That peace upon the earth shall be,
    Good-will henceforth with men belong.

In humble hearts,—no matter where,
    Nor what the fortune of their days,—
Hearts self-repressed in patient prayer,—
    Hearts all unworldly made by praise,—
Are depths of blessing purely fed
    By hidden force of changeless love,.
That make the life by mortals led
    Content as angel-life above.

E'en let it be that we must shed
    Sometimes the agonizing tear;
That past low mounds our feet are led,
    And we could wish the dead were here!

Let wars prevail, and scandal rave ;

    Let there be poverty and loss ;

But circumstance can not enslave,

    Nor peace be ruined by a cross.

The outward struggle, inward strife,

    Are meant for high development ;

We know what hand directs our life—

    The purpose of each incident.

And, knowing all, we murmur not,

    But bless the changeless, sure good-will

That portions to each separate lot'

    What best each separate vice may kill.

That pledges safety, but not ease ;

    Works by attrition, not by rust ;

And brings us on, by slow degrees,

    To perfect rest and higher trust.

We know the hand, we bless the will ;

    Come shade or shine, come tear or smile,

All things work good, and none bring ill,

    For love is near us all the while !

    7

So sing we, then, this festal night,
  The praise of Him who once for men
Assumed the burden and the blight,
  To give us Eden back again.
And this our carol should express—
  With this begin and with it cease—
He took our flesh our lives to bless;
  He bears our load, He gives us peace.

RELIGIOUS DIVISIONS.

> " Of old things, all are over-old ;
>   Of good things, none are good enough ;—
> We'll show that we can help to frame
>   A world of other stuff."
>
> WORDSWORTH.

I.

What might be done for earth, could man
    Irreverent notions put away,
    And feel he lives but to OBEY—
To forward Heaven's well-ordered plan !

What souls might be reclaimed and saved !
    What mental darkness, moral blight,
    Would be transfigured in the light
That shuns a heart by self depraved !

Our Lord is torn by wrangling sects—
    His Body mangled as of old ; *

* " The Church, which is His Body."—St. Paul.

Each sect is narrow, pinched, and cold,
    And none its wicked part suspects.

For each vaunts " progress," and asserts
      Its large improvement on the past;
      As if the best were always last,
    And time-worn things have least deserts.

As if what Christ himself contrived
      Might be amended, or improved,
      Or from its settled function moved,
    And into countless Hydras rived.

And feeling is put forth for right;
      Authority provokes a sneer;
      The times reject an overseer,
    Even if he have true heavenly might. ·

" Down with a hero ! " is the call :
      " Down with the priest, and them that rule !
      The formless mob shall be the school
    From whence we shape our dogmas all ! "

Thus the imperfect is a power
      That strives to mold what Christ began ;

And creeds are made to fit each man,
And fall an endless, dismal shower.

Dark, hungry souls that wait for truth
While parties wrangle and deceive,
Know not, alas ! what to believe,
And perish without hope or ruth.

But this is safe for me, I know :
To cleave to forms and doctrines old—
To grasp them with a firmer hold ;
For change is doubt, and doubt is woe.

II.

Thus wrote I but the other day,
And yet it was four years ago:
Time passes like the winds that blow—
So swift, so swift it hies away.

And with it passes hopes and fears—
Opinions pass, or suffer change ;
The soul attains a wider range,
And grows more tolerant with the years.
7*

For, after all, man is but man ;
    His views are blindness at the best :
    Not here are certainty and rest,
But truth has many sides. to scan.

The bird of passage, spring by spring,
    Comes back to the familiar nest ;
    For other home it makes no quest,
But there contented folds its wing.

And we, amid ancestral creeds
    Scarce questioned, mostly take a place,
    Presuming on God's equal grace,
And blind to many a truth that pleads

For our acceptance. 'Tis not well !
    But better far by *something* hold,
    Than filled with doubt and questions bold,
That savor of the deepest hell.

For One who yet shall come is Judge, .
    And knows of purpose, strength, and will ;
    He shall the faithful hope fulfil,
And His bestowals none shall grudge.

And He shall gather in His hands
    Time's tangled threads that crosswise run,
    And of His people make but one,
To serve Him in His heavenly lands.

III.

Above all names One Name is set ;
    The Crucified is King alone ;
    The great archangels at His throne
With humble reverence oft are met.

His lightest wish is their command ;
    They speed like lightning at His word ;
    By selfish preference undeterred,
Their movements all go hand in hand ;

And heaven is thus a heaven indeed,
    And all the worlds have certain peace ;
    But truth and harmony would cease,
Might every angel frame his creed,

Building on preference, or law
    Interpreted by his sole light—

Might each one do what seemed him right,
And individual inference draw.

One rule, and only one, controls
    The orbs that fill unmeasured space ;
    And scientists like action trace
In natural things between the poles.

Man only would ignore fixed bounds,
    Suiting his action to self-will—
    Would tasks self-born with might fulfil,
And leave undone what God propounds.

IV.

Divisions are the seed of death ;
    They change to comets peaceful stars,
    And desolate with hateful wars
All lands where sons of men draw breath.

God's kingdom is a bond of peace,
    And he who on its spirit feeds,
    Will leave untouched its simple creeds,
That faith and reverence may increase ;

That brotherhood be not a name,
  But substance felt in every heart;
  Since good men held by faith apart
Are ready soon with words of blame

And enginery of hate and blood.
  The principle of discord lies
  In what disorders and defies
The visible unity of the good.

Christ left His laws to loyal souls;
  He left His kingdom for their home;
  He built nor sect, nor papal Rome,
Nor gave His people separate goals;

But bade them harmonize, and strive
  In one sole house of charity,
  One kingdom of the bound but free—
Dead to themselves, to Him alive.

www.ingramcontent.com/pod-product-compliance
Lightning Source LLC
Chambersburg PA
CBHW020546270326
41927CB00006B/739